Road to the Free Digital Society.
Course Handbook

Vitaly Repin

June, 2015

ISBN 978-1514168288
Published by Vitaly Repin

Email: vitaly_repin@fsfe.org
Web: http://digitalfree.info

The book has been composed in LaTeX 2_ε.

Contents

1   Week 1. Introduction to the course. Human rights in Computing. Four Essential Freedoms. Patents   **5**

1.1   Introduction. Human rights in computing   6

1.2   Free Software and Four Freedoms. Free GNU/Linux distros. Malicious software   6

1.3   Computational idea patents and why they are bad. Real-life examples   6

1.4   Quiz 1   7

1.5   Human rights in computing. Mindmap   10

2   Week 2. Threats to the Free Digital Society   **11**

2.1   Digital Society: Inclusion or Escape? Surveillance, censorship, restricting the users   12

2.2   Threats from software that the user do not control   12

2.3   Threats from Service as a Software Substitute   13

2.4   War on Sharing. Precarity   13

2.5   Quiz 2   14

3   Week 3. Copyright and Copyleft: How to make software free?   **19**

3.1   Free Software Licenses. Introduction   20

3.2   GNU GPL and Affero GPL: Copyleft licenses   20

3.3   Non copyleft and weak copyleft licenses   21

3.4   Quiz 3   22

4   Week 4. Works of Authorship in the Free Digital Society. History, Philosophy, Practice   **25**

4.1   History of Copyright Law   26

4.2   Copyright in the digital age   27

4.3   Digital distribution: Ethical and Unethical   27

4.4   The Why, What and How of Creative Commons   28

4.5   Quiz 4   29

5 Week 5. Digital lifestyle to support freedom. How can we contribute to the Free Digital Society?   **31**

  5.1   Be careful which programs and services to use   32

  5.2   Use free software yourself   32

  5.3   Education and Free Software   33

  5.4   Make the Web Free   33

  5.5   Act to support Freedom   34

  5.6   Quiz 5   35

Appendices   37

A Answers to quizzes   **39**

  A.1   Quiz 1   40

  A.2   Quiz 2   40

  A.3   Quiz 3   41

  A.4   Quiz 4   42

  A.5   Quiz 5   43

B List of Abbreviations   **45**

C Index   **49**

CHAPTER 1

Introduction to the course.
Human rights in Computing.
Four Essential Freedoms.
Patents

1.1   Introduction. Human rights in computing

- Most important question to judge the program: What does it do for my freedom?
- Difference between free and proprietary software.
- Human rights in computing. Overview.

1.2   Free Software and Four Freedoms.
Free GNU/Linux distros.
Malicious software

- Software freedom: What is it?
- Four essentials freedoms:
    0. The freedom to run the program as you wish, for any purpose.
    1. The freedom to study how the program works, and change it so it does your computing as you wish.
    2. The freedom to redistribute copies so you can help your neighbor.
    3. The freedom to distribute copies of your modified versions to others.
- Why software freedoms are essential.
- GNU/Linux operating system. History and current status.
- Freedom as a goal. Free GNU/Linux distributions.
- Features of malicious software: Digital Restrictions Management (DRM) and Surveillance.
- How proprietary software is promoted by its victims: Skype example.
- Free software is a matter of liberty, not price.

1.3   Computational idea patents and why they are bad. Real-life examples

- What is computational idea patent?
- Why computational idea patents are bad?
    - Patents and copyrights are totally different things.
    - Analogy with music: imagine that there are musical idea patents (e.g., for melody).
    - Writing a program (as well as writing a symphony): combination of new and familiar ideas.

– Computational idea patents in real life: LZW and natural order recalculation examples.

1.4 Quiz 1

Question 1. What is the most important question to judge the program?

☐ How much does it cost to me (what is its total cost of ownership)?

☐ What does it do for my freedom?

☐ How buggy is it?

Question 2. If the program is not free we (FSF) call it ...

☐ Shareware.

☐ Proprietary.

☐ SaaSS.

Question 3. What is NOT one of the four freedoms?

☐ Run the program as you wish.

☐ Freedom to redistribute the program copies.

☐ Freedom to describe flaws in the program.

Question 4. What is the meaning of the acronym GNU?

☐ It it not an acronym. It's another name for the wildebeest.

☐ GNU's Not Unix.

☐ Good News Unlimited.

Question 5. Why Free Software Foundation (FSF) promotes the name "GNU/Linux" contrary to just "Linux"?

☐ The system some call "Linux" is the GNU system, combined with the kernel Linux.

☐ FSF wants GNU to be associated with Linux in order to get more power in protecting Software Freedoms.

☐ The question is wrong. FSF does not promote this name.

Question 6. Are all the GNU/Linux software distributions free?

☐ Yes. They are all free as in freedom. But some of them can be on sale because freedom is not about price at all.

☐ No. There is only one free GNU/Linux software distribution in the world and it is distributed by FSF. All other GNU/Linux software distros contain proprietary components and can not be defined as free.

☐ No. There are few free GNU/Linux software distributions. FSF promotes them.

Question 7. You wrote a program and in the process implemented an idea. After publishing your application you found that this idea had been patented previously (before you started to even think about it). What are the dangers?

☐ No danger because you have invented this idea independently from the patent owner.

☐ You can be sued by the patent owner. Your users can be sued also.

☐ You have committed a criminal offense described in the US penal code. There is a risk of being arrested by US police when you cross the USA border.

Question 8. What a supporter of free software is expected to think about an idea to use Skype as a collaboration tool and to put the Skype user id in his or her email signature?

☐ Sounds cool. I want to communicate with the people via Skype, a lot of my friends use it. I want them to know my Skype credentials as they will be able to use Skype to reach me.

☐ This idea is very bad. Skype is proprietary software and using it is a threat for the freedom. By putting my Skype username in the signature I will do even worse — I will promote the usage of the non-free software among the people I cooperate with.

☐ This idea sounds bad. Skype is owned by Microsoft and this corporation should be punished for their unethical behaviour and creation of the non-free software.

Question 9. What are the malicious features of Adobe Flash player?

☐ Digital Restrictions Management (DRM) and user surveillance feature where one site was able to write data into the Flash Player and another site could interrogate the Flash Player thus enabling sites to cross-identify a user.

☐ Digital Restrictions Management (DRM) and adware.

☐ Adobe Flash Player constantly reports the user's IP address to the Adobe headquarters.

Question 10. Imagine that in order to promote the progress of symphonic music the European governments of XVIII century established a patent system on music themes. How would it influence the work of composers?

- ☐ Composers would become richer and would be able to be more creative because of the need to invent the new themes in the music all the time.

- ☐ No influence at all.

- ☐ It would be harder for composers to create rich symphonies because every new piece of art reuses the ideas developed by previous artists in one way or the other

1.5 Human rights in computing. Mindmap

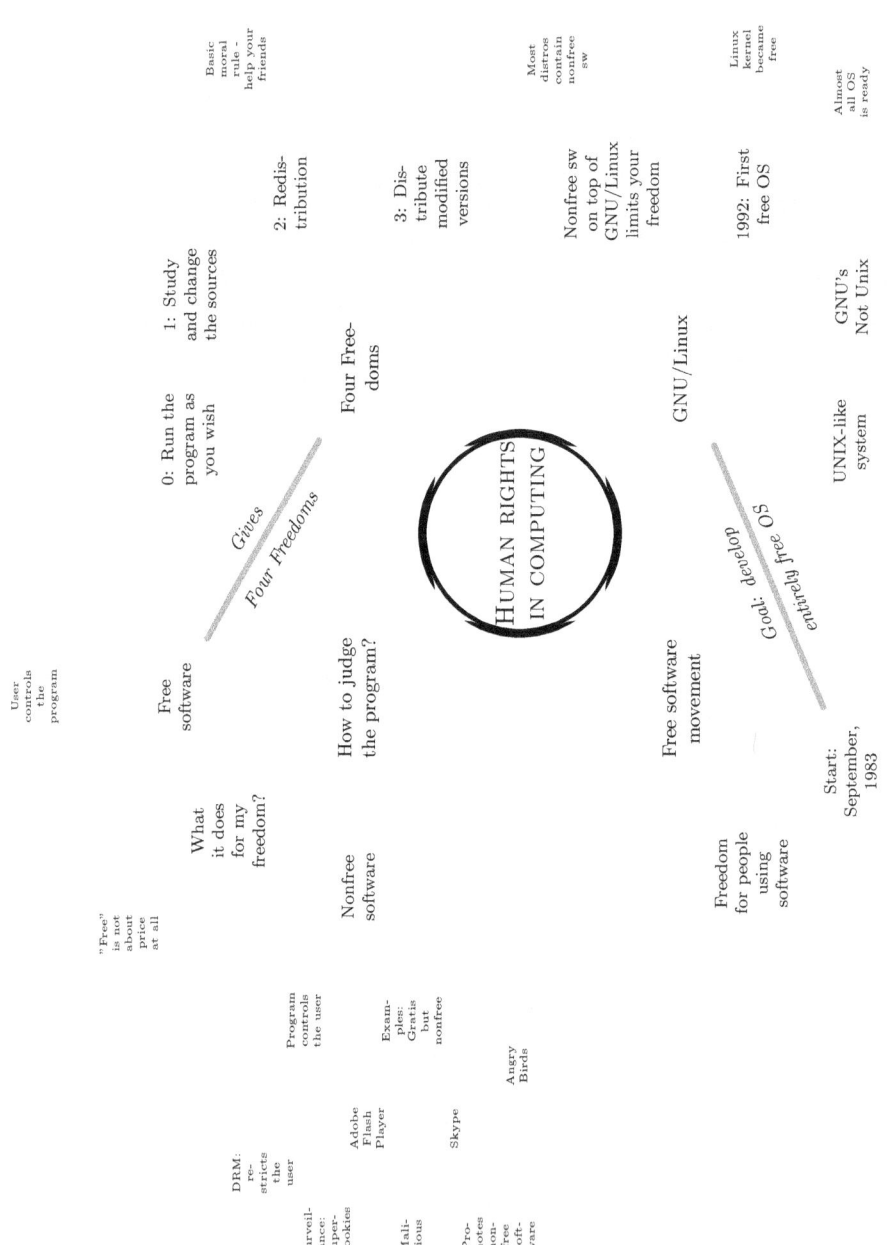

CHAPTER 2

THREATS TO
THE FREE DIGITAL SOCIETY

2.1 Digital Society: Inclusion or Escape? Surveillance, censorship, restricting the users

- Shall we aim for inclusion to or escape from the Digital Society?
- What are the threats to the Digital Society? Overview.
- Threat 1: Surveillance.

  - Surveillance and Democracy: how are they compatible?
  - Who watches the watchmen? Why society needs whistleblowers.
  - Common engineering practice of the day: keep all the data you can.
  - Three ways to spy on people. Examples and the ways to react:
    * Through their own systems.
    * Through the systems they use but don't own (e.g., phone networks).
    * Surveillance systems which are designed specifically for this activity.
  - Data from business surveillance systems is available to the state.

- Threat 2: Censorship.

  - Censorship in Internet: "filtration".
  - Country examples (Europe, Asia, ...).
  - Propaganda methods: using disgusting things (e.g., child pornography) to advocate censorship tools.

- Threat 3: Data formats that restrict their users.

  - Digital handcuffs.
  - DRM: Digital Restrictions Management.
  - Reasons why secret data formats exist.

2.2 Threats from software that the user do not control

- There are only two options: the users controls the program OR the program controls the users.
- Backdoors and Universal Backdoors.
- Real-life examples: Amazon Swindle, portable phones.

2.3   Threats from Service as a Software Substitute

- SaaSS: new way to lose control over your computing.
- SaaSS: how it works. Technical explanation.
- SaaSS is equivalent to running non-free program with universal backdoor which makes it proprietary malware.
- Paradoxical relationships between SaaSS and free/non-free software.
  - If server software is free, it does not help the users. It benefits only the server owner.
  - If server software is non-free then server owner does not control it. Somebody else controls it. The users do not benefit in either of the situations.
- Not all the services are SaaSS:
  - Sometimes you can't fully control your computing — e.g., when you are communicating with other people.
  - If your task can be done if you have powerful computer and required software, then server-based solution is SaaSS. Otherwise it is not.
- Examples of SaaSS: Translation and Speech Recognition services.

2.4   War on Sharing. Precarity

- What is sharing and why it is good.
- Attack on sharing is an attack on social cooperation.
- Two kinds of works:
  - Works we need to do practical jobs (e.g. reference works, educational works): should be free.
  - Others (e.g. entertainment, opinion, art) should be freely shareable.
- Ways to attack sharing:
  - Laws which forbid sharing.
  - Propaganda. Terms like "Piracy" and "Theft":
  - Reject propaganda terms! Attacking ship is very bad, sharing is good.
  - Legally speaking, copyright infringement is never theft. Sometimes it's a crime, sometimes not. But is it NEVER a theft.
  - Publishing of the works using secret formats with the purpose to restrict the public:

- DVD "conspiracy": if you want to manufacture DVD player, you need to join the conspiracy. No competition in this important part of DVD player functionality!

- DMCA: Digital Millennium Copyright Act:

    * Banning distribution of free software which allows to read DVDs in the secret format.

    * Similar laws in EU and other countries.

- DRM: Digital Restrictions Management:

    * Introduced by AACS (Advanced Access Content System) "conspiracy".

    * Example of AACS power: they managed to ban analog video outputs.

- Disconnect people from Internet when they are *accused* of sharing (without a trial):

    * Crashing of the basic principle of justice — no punishment without a trial.

- Controlling what our technology does is a worse attack on society than controlling prices. It shall be treated as more grave crime.

- Usage of Internet is precarious:

    - You need to cooperate with ISP, DNS registrar, other companies in order to do your tasks.

    - Typically the contracts you sign are so, that they can be canceled for any reason by service provider.

    - Example: Dirty Tricks campaign against WikiLeaks.

    - Analogy: imagine that government convinces your phone or electrical company that it's in their interest to stop serving you.

    - Regulation is needed like for other public utilities: no right to disconnect if I pay according to the contract, no way to discriminate single customer etc.

2.5   Quiz 2

Question 1. Is it a good or bad thing to participate in the digital society? Select one answer.

☐ Yes, sure. New digital technologies improve people's living conditions dramatically and we should do our best to let everybody to benefit from the new technologies.

☐ No, not at all. New digital technologies make the people less smart, they restrict abilities of the human brain to think. We need to avoid them and focus on developing our brains instead.

☐ It depends on how digital society is set up and how does it respect people's freedom.

Question 2. Which of the following is NOT an example of surveillance threat to the people's freedom?

☐ Systems to record the user's location using the data from GSM or CDMA base stations where user's phone was registered.

☐ Portable GPS tracker gadget which tracks your geo-location and stores it in its memory. GPS track can be downloaded from the gadget through USB or RS-232 interfaces.

☐ Companies monitoring the behavior of their users via web sites (e.g., cookies) for advertising purposes.

Question 3. Several examples of censorship in different countries were presented in the video. Which country was NOT mentioned in this context?

☐ Turkey

☐ Finland

☐ Saudi Arabia

Question 4. What are "digital handcuffs"?

☐ Modern handcuffs for the prisoners with escape records. They have surveillance functionality implemented using CDMA technology.

☐ The situation when software users are restricted by the secret data format which prevents data interchange with some of the other programs.

☐ The situation when the user is forced to use the proprietary software because there is no free software with the similar functionality available.

Question 5. "Software as a Service Substitute" means losing the control on your computing as it is done on somebody's else server. What is the difference between Wikipedia and Speech Recognition services from end-user point of view?

☐ No difference. Both process user's data on their side and both should be avoided because the users is loosing the control on his/her computing.

☐ By contributing to Wikipedia the user helps it to do its computing and this is expected by the user. By using Speech Recognition service user's own computing is done by the server.

☐ Wikipedia is a service to share the data with other users in a free way. Speech Recognition service is proprietary solution therefore it is bad idea to use it.

Question 6. What is mr. Stallman's opinion on the piracy? Select the best answer.

☐ Attacking ships is bad. But it has nothing in common with sharing which is good. It's morally bad to try to associate something which is good (sharing) with something which is bad (attacking ships).

☐ Piracy is a good thing and we should all be pirates. It is in the nature of the human being to share things.

☐ Piracy is sometimes good and sometimes bad. It depends on the nature of the works which are shared (e.g., sharing of the fiction books can be sometimes considered bad while sharing of the engineering books is always good).

Question 7. What Precarity threat is about?

☐ Everybody needs to be educated about the dangers of the digital society but in reality only the minor percentage of the population has this knowledge.

☐ Any activity in the Internet requires cooperation from a lot of stakeholders — ISP, hosting providers etc. Governments can use these stakeholders to disconnect the service (e.g., web site) they don't like from the Internet by putting pressure on those stakeholders. It is possible because a lot of service providers have a freedom to break the contract with the user in any time.

☐ Children are becoming the victims of the violent content accessible in the Internet. As a result, school shooting occur. New policy towards the way children can use Internet should be developed.

Question 8. What is "universal backdoor"? Select one answer.

☐ The interface through which somebody else than the user can install any software changes in the user's system without user's permission.

☐ Method of bypassing normal authentication, securing unauthorized remote access to a computer, obtaining access to plaintext, and so on, while attempting to remain undetected.

☐ The name of the method to unencrypt DRM-protected movies in some of DVD players.

Question 9. Which parts of "dirty tricks" campaign against WikiLeaks was discussed in the lectures?

☐ CIA used sexual entrapment against Julian Assange.

☐ US government tried to convince the companies which provided services to WikiLeaks (e.g., eCommerce services) that it's in their best interests to stop serve WikiLeaks.

☐ Governments run defamation campaign against WikiLeaks trying to portrait it as untrustworthy source of information.

Question 10. Why SaaSS is an equivalent of proprietary malware? Select one answer.

☐ If you use SaaSS your computing is done by the server. Server owner can misuse your data.

☐ SaaSS has the same effect as running non free programs with universal backdoor (because server owner can change server software in any time and it changes the way user's computing is done).

☐ SaaSS is proprietary solution. Proprietary solution is always malware.

CHAPTER 3

COPYRIGHT AND COPYLEFT: HOW TO MAKE SOFTWARE FREE?

3.1   Free Software Licenses. Introduction

- Why does a free program have a license?

  - Everything which is written (including programs) have a license auto-matically. "Default" (silent) license does not allow people to modify and distribute programs.

  - Typical proprietary license: a contract which restricts users even more than copyright laws.

  - Free software license: gives back to the users their rights which were taken by copyright laws.

- Copyleft and non copyleft free software licenses.

  - In order for the license to be free software license it shall give the users four essential freedoms (see lecture 1.2). There are many ways to do it which explains why there are many free software licenses.

  - Big dichotomy among free software licenses: copyleft and non copyleft.

  - Copyleft does not allow the user to take free software and make it non free (even after making modifications to the software).

    * The problem is real. E.g., TeX. Its UNIX implementation was made non free while original Knuth's implementation was free (but dis-tributed under non copyleft license).

    * Copyleft idea: to give the freedom to the "next" users of the program.

3.2   GNU GPL and Affero GPL: Copyleft licenses

- GNU General Public License: GPL.

  - Copyleft license

  - Originally GPL was developed as a license to distribute GNU system un-der. GPL 3 is designed for other kind of work also.

  - GPL prohibits a lot of different means to make free software non-free. Examples:

    * *Release only binaries.* GPL requires source code to be available.

    * *Change of the license.* GPL requires to keep the license.

    * *Patent.* It's not allowed to use patents to limit the freedom of software distributed under GPL.

- Other free software licenses are non copyleft. Some of them are very weak ("pushover licenses" allow almost everything). There are also weak copyleft licenses. E.g., Mozilla Public License (MPL):

  - Files which were received under MPL shall be distributed under the same license (MPL) but new files can be added with different license.

- Way to make free software non free: add new source code files under other license and call the new subroutines defined there from original files.

- GNU Affero General Public License: AGPL.

  - Secondary effect of copyleft: because modifications are free, developer of the original version cat take them and incorporate to the original software. This is the way to contribute to the community's shared knowledge.

  - Installing modified GPL software on the server is not its distribution. Hence, it's not needed to make the source code available. Therefore second effect of copyleft does not work.

  - AGPL addresses this problem. It requires source code to be available if the software runs on server and is available to others.

  - Relation to SaaSS (see also lecture 2.3):

    * No contradiction with "SaaSS is bad" logic: there are many server software which is not SaaSS and which needs AGPL protection.

    * No license can make SaaSS ethical. The only way to solve the problem is to take server code and execute it by the user.

3.3 Non copyleft and weak copyleft licenses

- Sometimes there are advantages in using non copyleft license.

  - *Ogg/Vorbis player.* It was considered as very important for all music players to be able to support this free format. That's why Ogg/Vorbis codec was distributed under non copyleft license: Apache 2.0 License.

  - Recommended non copyleft license to use: Apache 2.0. Reason: patent protection

- BSD licenses: original and modified (revised):

  - These licenses are very different. Don't state "The code is distributed under BSD license". The question is — *which* BSD license?

  - Important difference: advertising requirements.

  - Original BSD license is not recommended to be used to distribute new software under.

- Other free software licenses:

  - X11, Expat licenses are not "MIT licenses". They are different licenses. Refer to each one specifically.

  - FSF: Various Licenses and Comments about them

  - FSF: How to choose a license for your own work

3.4   Quiz 3

Question 1. What is the primary purpose of free software license?

☐ To allow free distribution of modifications made to the free software. Therefore to contribute to the community's shared knowledge.

☐ To give the user back their freedom taken by copyright law.

☐ To free the developers of the software from any obligations and claims which can be risen by their users.

Question 2. Which problem is addressed by Affero GPL which is not in scope of GPL?

☐ If the modified software is executed in the server and is used by others, modifications of the server software shall also be available to those "others".

☐ Software libraries distributed under GPL force the packages which use them to be licensed under GPL as well. AGPL addresses this issue by making copyleft conditions weaker than in original GPL.

☐ GNU system needed non copyleft licenses to accompany copyleft (which is GPL) because some of the GNU projects wanted to use non copyleft licenses. AGPL is an answer to this demand.

Question 3. Is Mozilla Public License (MPL) a copyleft and why? Select one answer.

☐ Yes. It makes it impossible to make free program non free.

☐ No. It is possible to make free program non free if original program is released under MPL.

☐ Yes. Because it requires the original source code to be distributed under MPL license as well.

Question 4. Which non copyleft license is recommended by FSF to be used with projects which needs to be distributed under non copyleft freesoftware license?

☐ X11 License.

☐ Apache 2.0 License.

☐ GNU AGPL.

Question 5. What was the reason for distribution Ogg/Vorbis codec under non copyleft license?

☐ It was very important to extend the range of music players supporting Ogg/Vorbis format.

☐ It was decided to test and measure the effect of selecting non copyleft license on software distribution coverage.

☐ It was a huge mistake — developers of the codec were not aware of the disadvantages of non copyleft licenses as explained in our lectures.

Question 6. What is called "Secondary Effect of Copyleft"?

☐ Copyleft gives users the Second Freedom — the freedom to study how the program works, and change it so it does their computing as they wish.

☐ Copyleft prohibits limiting users freedom and as secondary effect proprietary software developers don't like to use and modify the software which is distributed under copyleft.

☐ Modifications to the program distributed under copyleft license can be included into the original program. Therefore copyleft facilitates contribution to the communitys shared knowledge.

Question 7. What is called "pushover license" and why?

☐ These free software licenses are very weak non copyleft licenses. They are called this way because they permit almost everything.

☐ This is another name for copyleft licenses. It emphasizes the fact that these licenses are pushing the freedom to the users.

☐ This name is used for proprietary licenses. It emphasizes the fact that proprietary software is pushed to the users with the help of these licenses.

Question 8. I want to become SaaSS user. Server code is distributed under AGPL. Am I safe?

☐ Yes. Because server code is distributed under free software license and I have access to the server software source code.

☐ No. No license can make SaaSS ethical. My computing is still done by the server and my privacy is under threat, for example.

☐ No. AGPL is not a license which can be used to protect the users from SaaSS. Other license (which is mentioned in the additional materials for this course) shall be used to achieve this effect.

Question 9. Why it's a bad idea to state in the source code "This source code is distributed under BSD license"? Select one answer.

☐ There is more than one BSD license. It's better to be specific.

☐ It's not enough to make such a one-line statement. I need to include the text of the license in every source code file.

☐ Because in this case all the users of this software will need to mention "Berkley University" in all the advertisings of their products (based on this software).

Question 10. What happens if I publish my software without any license?

☐ My software will give freedom to the users. They will exercise four essential freedoms described in the lecture 1.2.

☐ My software will be in so called "public domain". Hence, it will give freedom to the users.

☐ My software will be automatically copyrighted. Others will not be able to exercise all the four essential freedoms described in the lecture 1.2.

CHAPTER 4

WORKS OF AUTHORSHIP IN THE FREE DIGITAL SOCIETY. HISTORY, PHILOSOPHY, PRACTICE

4.1   History of Copyright Law

- Our basic principles are deep, technology is superficial. But it can make the very same act more or less good.

- Copying in the ancient world:

    - Slow and inefficient.

    - No economy of scale.

    - Required skills: only reading and writing.

    - Required equipment: only "equipment" needed to read and write.

    - Decentralized system of copying. Nothing like copyright law.

- Copyright and censorship were closely related throughout the history.

- Copying in the age of printing press:

    - Economy of scale.

    - Special expensive equipment is required.

    - Special skills (very different from reading and writing) are needed to operate printing press.

    - Centralized system of copying. Beginning of copyright.

- Beginning of copyright. Copyright as a tool for industrial regulation:

    - Appeared in England in XVI century.

    - Started from perpetual monopoly to publish certain book. Changed in XVII century: monopoly to an author (not a publisher!) for 14 years. Could be renewed once if the author was still alive.

    - Idea of copyright: scheme which encourages writing.

    - US Constitution (1788) allows congress to create a copyright system with the purpose to promote progress. Copyright can not be perpetual, only time-limited.

- In the age of printing press copyright was used as an industry regulation tool. It regulated publishers and was controlled by authors. Copyright law was:

    - *Mostly uncontroversial* because it restricted the publishers and not the readers. If you are not a publisher, you don't have strong reasons to object.

    - *Easy to enforce* because it was easy to understand who published certain book. No need to visit every reader to enforce the copyright law.

    - *Beneficial for the society* — public traded part of its natural rights which it did not exercised to the real benefit — more books written.

4.2   Copyright in the digital age

- Computer networks — new advance in the technology of copying.
- Copying became more effective and benefit of printing press in mass production almost disappeared.
- Situation now reminds antiquity with the difference in efficiency of copying.
- Copyright law now restricts everyone and controlled mostly by the publishers in the name of authors.
- The reasons copyright was beneficial for society in the age of printing press are not valid anymore:
  - *No more uncontroversial* because now it restricts everybody, not only publishers.
  - *Not easy to enforce* because the copyright law shall be enforced against everyone.
  - *No longer beneficial.* Public wants its natural rights back because now we are able to exercise them.
- Changes in copyright practices:
  - Wave of copyright time extensions all over the world. Examples:
    * EU: extended copyright time for sound records and textual work.
    * USA: Mickey mouse copyright act (20 years extension of copyright time).
  - Real reasons to extend copyright time — companies had valuable rights which were about to expire.
  - We are on a way to perpetual copyright with constant extension of copyright law.
  - Mexico example: copyright validity time is 100 years after author's death.
  - Previously copyright was an exception and not a general rule. Not anymore. Publishers try to have total control over public through digital technologies (Digital Restrictions Management).
  - Attempts to take total control over public are made with non-free software — it's not possible to do this with the help of free software.

4.3   Digital distribution: Ethical and Unethical

- What is wrong with Amazon "Swindle"?
- "Swindle" is an appropriate name for Amazon's e-reader because it swindles readers out of the traditional freedoms of readers:

- *Freedom to buy a book anonymously.* Amazon requires its readers to identify themselves and maintain a list with the books which were read by the user. Existence of this list is dangerous for the fundamental human rights. But Swindle also reports to Amazon the pages which are read, sends notes and highlights to Amazon. Swindle is a complete surveillance of reading device.

- *Freedom to give a book to a friend, to sell it through used book store.* Swindle End User License Agreement (EULA) rejects an idea of property — the book is owned by Amazon, not by the user! "Swindle" DRM and EULA together swindle readers out of this right.

- *Freedom to keep a book as long as you wish.* Amazon can remotely delete books from Swindle and was doing it already ("1984" case).

- Swindle has universal backdoor (autoupgrade, see lecture 2.2) which means additional restrictions can be installed later by Amazon.

- Swindle is not the only malicious e-reader device: most of other e-readers are doing a lot of snooping too.

- Requirements to be met in order for digital distribution to be ethical:

  - No DRM (Digital Restrictions Management).

  - No EULA — books shall be your property.

  - Possibility to purchase anonymously.

- Currently in most cases distribution of digital copies over Internet is ethically worse than distribution of physical copies.

- The same problems arise with audio and video (e.g., DRM is used with streaming services).

4.4 The Why, What and How of Creative Commons

- Different Creative Commons (CC) licenses give more or less freedoms:

  - Six main CC licenses. Two of them are free.

  - CC BY — push over license. CC BY SA — copyleft license.

  - Four other CC licenses are non-free. E.g., NC license restricts commercial usage and ND license restricts modification.

- Which CC license to use for the project?

  - For statements of opinion, artistic works non-free licenses are OK.

  - If the works shall be free (e.g., practical work, reference, educational) — use one of two free CC licenses.

- License choice is crucial — don't delay this decision until the end of the project. Agree with project team in the very beginning!

- "This work is distributed under CC license" — confusing statement. *Which* CC license? It makes a lot of difference.

- Never distribute software under CC license! See lecture 3 for software licenses information.

4.5 Quiz 4

Question 1. Select correct statements about system of copying in antiquity:

- ☐ It had no economy of scale.
- ☐ It was decentralized.
- ☐ It was subject to copyright regulation.

Question 2. Which statement about copying system in the age of printing press is NOT correct?

- ☐ It had economy of scale.
- ☐ It was subject to copyright regulation.
- ☐ It was decentralized.

Question 3. When copyright began?

- ☐ In the antiquity.
- ☐ In age of a printing press.
- ☐ We were not able to trace the origins of copyright in the history.

Question 4. Why copyright system was mostly uncontroversial in the age of a printing press?

- ☐ It was easy to enforce.
- ☐ It was beneficial for society.
- ☐ It restricted only limited amount of people — publishers.

Question 5. Is it easy to enforce copyright system in our times and why? Select the answer which is closest to what was stated in the lecture:

- ☐ It is not easy because it shall be enforced against everyone which requires invading people's homes, computers and Internet connections.
- ☐ It is not easy because the copyright law is no more uncontroversial and a lot of people stop to respect it.
- ☐ It is easy because modern day technology (e.g. DRM / digital handcuffs) are used extensively nowadays.

Question 6. Which conditions shall be met in order for distribution of digital copies to be ethical? Select all that apply:

☐ No DRM.

☐ No EULA.

☐ Copies shall be distributed under one of free licenses (e.g., CC BY, CC BY SA or GFDL).

☐ Distributor shall use only free software to distribute the copies.

☐ Ability to purchase anonymously

Question 7. Which Creative Commons licenses are free? Select all the apply:

☐ Attribution-ShareAlike 4.0 International (CC BY-SA 4.0).

☐ Attribution-NonCommercial 4.0 International (CC BY-NC 4.0).

☐ Attribution 4.0 International (CC BY 4.0).

Question 8. Which of the following licenses are OK for artistic works but are not good for practical works?

☐ Attribution 4.0 International (CC BY 4.0)

☐ Attribution-NonCommercial 4.0 International (CC BY-NC 4.0)

☐ Attribution-NoDerivatives 4.0 International (CC BY-ND 4.0)

Question 9. Somebody asks you to participate in a project and tells that results of this project (e.g., photos you made) will be distributed under Creative Commons license. You want the project results to be free. What is better to clarify first? Select all that apply:

☐ Which CC license will be used?

☐ Will you use only free software in order to execute the project and publish it?

☐ Will the results of the project be not only free (as in "freedom") but also gratuitous for the public?

Question 10. Why copyright was beneficial for society in times when it was used as a tool for industrial regulation? Select the best answer:

☐ It was easy to enforce copyright

☐ Public traded away certain parts of its natural rights that ordinary people were not exercising and in exchange got real benefits of more books being written'

☐ It was mostly uncontroversial

Digital lifestyle to support freedom. How can we contribute to the Free Digital Society?

5.1   Be careful which programs and services to use

- Facebook is a monstrous surveillance engine.

  - Facebook does surveillance on its useds and not useds as well. Call them "useds" rather than "users" because Facebook is using them, not vice versa.

  - Publishing somebody's photo in Facebook is treating him or her badly. Exception — public events.

- Distribute data in formats favorable to the free software.

  - Ogg/Vorbis, Webm. NO MP*, NO Flash, NO quicktime and other non-free formats.

  - If your hardware records the data in non-free format convert files to the free formats before distributing.

  - Make sure the platform you use to distribute the files does not lead the users to use non-free software (e.g., YouTube has non-free JavaScript and Flash).

- Carefully select the programs and devices you use: avoid DRM, spyware, malware, proprietary jails.

- Don't use products that steal your freedom. E.g., Amazon "Swindle".

- Mobile phones — mobile computers with outstanding surveillance capabilities. Stalin's dream.

- Protect your personal data — it can be misused! (e.g., wi-fi access which requires your identity).

5.2   Use free software yourself

- Free GNU/Linux distributions:

  - List of Free Linux Distributions: BLAG, gNewSense etc

  - Well-known GNU/Linux distros continue to have non-free software!

- Non-free parts in Linux: firmware. Binaries masqueraded as source-code.

- Free GNU/Linux distributions contain only free software (hence, do not contain non-free firmware). As a result not all the hardware works.

- Tolerate inconvenience if your aim is freedom. Otherwise you will lose your freedom.

- Reject proprietary software. No matter how useful it is.

- Prefer releasing no program to releasing proprietary program. Reason: releasing proprietary program harms society. If you do not release program at all you don't harm society at least.

- Free Software Directory

5.3 Education and Free Software

- Four reasons to use free software in education:

  1. *Saving money.* Most superficial reason. Proprietary software companies started to give gratis or nearly gratis copies of their software to the educational institutions.

  2. *Educational system should not make society depending on the proprietary software.* Schools shall reject gratis copies of proprietary software for the same reasons they reject free samples of addictive drugs for the students.

  3. *Education of best programmers.* If software is proprietary student can't study its source code and education is not possible. Studying how to program is not studying how to write small programs. Students shall start from writing small parts in large programs. Free software gives this opportunity.

  4. *Ethical education. Education in citizenship.* Schools teach above all to the spirit of good will, habit to help the neighbor. Schools shall give examples of ethical behavior. Which is not possible with proprietary software.

- Students and teachers — pressure your school to move to the free software:

  - Make the people aware that usage of non-free software is wrong.

  - If you are student and you have a class where proprietary software is used stand up in the very first lecture and ask to help you to find a way to make the work of this class with only free software. Explain that you are ready to work harder and understand possible inconveniences.

  - Your readiness to inconveniences shows that you are serious about freedom and influences other people around you.

5.4 Make the Web Free

- The JavaScript Trap:

  - Web servers load to your browser JavaScript programs. Typically they execute them silently — without letting the users know.

  - Many of these programs are non-free

- GNU LibreJS: Free JavaScript in your browser:

- Free add-on for Mozilla-based browsers (e.g., Firefox).

- Checks all JavaScript code which is about to be executed by the browser. Blocks the code if it is non-trivial or non-free. Informs the user about blocked JavaScript in the page.

- GNU LibreJS makes it easy to complain about non-free JavaScript to the web masters. It extracts web masters contact information from the page and shows a special "Complain" button to the user.

- It's very important to complain about non-free JavaScript code to contribute to FSF cause.

• The JavaScript Developers Task Force:

  - To make sure that all the JavaScript executed in the browser is free is only a first step.

  - Need to be able to easily change the code and exchange it with others. Challenging task.

• Switch to free browser: GNU IceCat:

  - Mozilla-based.

  - Removed Firefox name and logo because they have imposed non-free restrictions.

  - Extensions list: modified in such a way that only free extensions are listed.

  - Does not send the addresses you've visited to google (privacy).

  - Tracking mechanisms are blocked (e.g., Facebook "Like" button, Google analytics etc).

  - LibreJS is active by default.

5.5   Act to support Freedom

• Celebrate Freedom Fighters.

  - Edward Snowden is a hero. Many people are trying to demonise him. It's important to celebrate him and the people like him.

• Warn your friends about dangerous products.

  - Example: Amazon Kindle. It makes people antisocial, divides them. Make sure your friends know this before they decide to use this product.

• Promote free software in your educational institution:

  - It's your responsibility to campaign for free software in your educational institution!

  - Setting up reverse engineering classes is very important. We need to operate the hardware with secret specifications without non-free software.

- Reject propaganda terms:
  - E.g., "Piracy", "Theft". It is not right to call Sharing this way (see also lecture 2.4 "War on Sharing").
  - Good way to reject propaganda is to use jokes and humor. E.g., "Piracy? Attacking ships is very bad. Movie piracy? Pirates of the Caribbean is a good movie".
- Join Defective by Design movement:
  - More about Digital Restrictions Management (DRM) — see in the lecture 2.4 "War on Sharing".
  - This campaign shall be big. Don't expect that the battle will be won without you.
- Upgrade from Windows! It's not possible to live in freedom with Windows. Any version of Windows. Don't downgrade to Windows Vista at least.
- Learn how to make easy changes:
  - Anybody can exercise Freedoms 0 and 2 (see lecture 1.2) — *the freedom to run the program as you wish, for any purpose* and *the freedom to redistribute copies so you can help your neighbor.*
  - Freedoms 1 and 3 (see lecture 1.2: *the freedom to study how the program works, and change it so it does your computing as you wish* and *the freedom to distribute copies of your modified versions to others*) require programming skills.
  - It's useful to learn how to make easy changes in the software. You don't need to become software engineer in order to be able to do them. Analogy: it's useful to know how to make small maintenance of your car even if you are not a professional mechanic.

5.6   Quiz 5

Question 1. Dr. Stallman tells: "Linux in its usual version contains non-free software". What does he refer to? Select the best answer:

- ☐ Non-free applications which can be found in the popular GNU/Linux distributions.
- ☐ Non-free firmware "blobs" which can be found in Linux kernel.
- ☐ Software included into most of the (non-free) GNU/Linux distributions which deals with proprietary data formats (e.g., Adobe Flash).

Question 2. Which of the following reasons was NOT stated among the reasons to use only free software in education?

☐ Ethical education. Education in citizenship.

☐ Educational system should not make society depending on the proprietary software.

☐ Education system serves public interest therefore it shall not be favourable to any business.

☐ Education of best programmers.

Question 3. Which features GNU LibreJS has? Select all answers that are correct:

☐ It blocks JavaScript code if it is either non-trivial or non-free.

☐ It makes it easier to complain about non-free JavaScript to web masters.

☐ It collects information about most often blocked JavaScript non-free code and can send it to GNU LibreJS developes. The goal is to find most used non-free JavaScript code in the net.

Question 4. Which features GNU IceCat has? Select all answers that are correct:

☐ It blocks Google Analytics.

☐ It maintains list of free add-ons.

☐ It contains LibreJS extension to address the JavaScript problem known as "Javascript Trap".

Question 5. You have video-recorded a public event. Your camera have saved video as MPEG4 file. What is the best strategy to distribute the video?

☐ Publish the file I have got from the camera on any of the popular services for video hosting.

☐ Convert the file to Ogg Vorbis or webm format and find the service to publish it. This service shall deliver video to the users in the format favourable to the free software and should not lead its users to use non-free programs (e.g., non-free JavaScript).

☐ This video can not be distributed at all because it was recorded with non-free defected-by-design video camera.

Question 6. Which of the following statements about free GNU/Linux distributions are WRONG?

☐ They are well-known.

☐ They are more convenient than non-free GNU/Linux distributions.

☐ They do not contain non-free software, backdoors, DRM, malware and spyware inside.

Question 7. Why is it important to celebrate freedom fighters? Select the best answer:

- ☐ We need to show to the Big Brother that we are careful about freedom and respect those who are fighting for it.

- ☐ There people and powerful organizations which are trying to demonise freedom fighters.That's why it's especially important to state that they are heroes who are fighting for our freedom.

- ☐ We want them to realize that they have done really great things for us. It's our moral obligation to say "thank you!" to our heroes.

Question 8. How free software helps to teach programming? Select all the answers that are correct:

- ☐ It makes it possible to study source code.

- ☐ It makes it possible to write small changes in the big programs.

- ☐ By studying free software source code the student can know what is bad coding style and how he or she shall not write programs.

Question 9. What is "Defective By Design" about? Select the best answer:

- ☐ Dr. Stallman names Windows operating system in such a way

- ☐ Name for all non-free software used by FSF. This software is defective by design because it is designed to exercise unjust power over the users.

- ☐ Campaign exposing DRM-encumbered devices and media for what they really are. Supporters are working together to eliminate DRM as a threat to innovation in media, the privacy of readers, and freedom for computer users.

Question 10. What is proprietary jail? Select the best answer:

- ☐ US prison operated by private company.

- ☐ Proprietary systems that are jails — they do not allow the user to freely install applications. These systems are platforms for censorship imposed by the company that owns the system.

- ☐ FreeBSD jail mechanism (implementation of operating system-level virtualization that allows administrators to partition a system into several independent mini-systems called jails) used in some of Android and Apple devices.

APPENDIX A

ANSWERS TO QUIZZES

A.1 Quiz 1

Solution 1. What does it do for my freedom?

Solution 2. Proprietary.

Solution 3. Freedom to describe flaws in the program.

Solution 4. GNU's Not Unix.

Solution 5. The system some call "Linux" is the GNU system, combined with the kernel Linux.

Solution 6. No. There are few free GNU/Linux software distributions. FSF promotes them.

Solution 7. You can be sued by the patent owner. Your users can be sued also.

Solution 8. This idea is very bad. Skype is proprietary software and using it is a threat for the freedom. By putting my Skype username in the signature I will do even worse — I will promote the usage of the non-free software among the people I cooperate with.

Solution 9. Digital Restrictions Management (DRM) and user surveillance feature where one site was able to write data into the Flash Player and another site could interrogate the Flash Player thus enabling sites to cross-identify a user.

Solution 10. It would be harder for composers to create rich symphonies because every new piece of art reuses the ideas developed by previous artists in one way or the other

A.2 Quiz 2

Solution 1. It depends on how digital society is set up and how does it respect people's freedom.

Solution 2. Portable GPS tracker gadget which tracks your geo-location and stores it in its memory. GPS track can be downloaded from the gadget through USB or RS-232 interfaces.

Solution 3. Saudi Arabia

Solution 4. The situation when software users are restricted by the secret data format which prevents data interchange with some of the other programs.

Solution 5. By contributing to Wikipedia the user helps it to do its computing and this is expected by the user. By using Speech Recognition service user's own computing is done by the server.

Solution 6. Attacking ships is bad. But it has nothing in common with sharing which is good. It's morally bad to try to associate something which is good (sharing) with something which is bad (attacking ships).

Solution 7. Any activity in the Internet requires cooperation from a lot of stake-holders — ISP, hosting providers etc. Governments can use these stakeholders to disconnect the service (e.g., web site) they don't like from the Internet by putting pressure on those stakeholders. It is possible because a lot of service providers have a freedom to break the contract with the user in any time.

Solution 8. The interface through which somebody else than the user can install any software changes in the user's system without user's permission.

Solution 9. US government tried to convince the companies which provided services to WikiLeaks (e.g., eCommerce services) that it's in their best interests to stop serve WikiLeaks.

Solution 10. SaaSS has the same effect as running non free programs with universal backdoor (because server owner can change server software in any time and it changes the way user's computing is done).

A.3 Quiz 3

Solution 1. To give the user back their freedom taken by copyright law.

Solution 2. If the modified software is executed in the server and is used by others, modifications of the server software shall also be available to those "others".

Solution 3. No. It is possible to make free program non free if original program is released under MPL.

Solution 4. Apache 2.0 License.

Solution 5. It was very important to extend the range of music players supporting Ogg/Vorbis format.

Solution 6. Modifications to the program distributed under copyleft license can be included into the original program. Therefore copyleft facilitates contribution to the communitys shared knowledge.

Solution 7. These free software licenses are very weak non copyleft licenses. They are called this way because they permit almost everything.

Solution 8. No. No license can make SaaSS ethical. My computing is still done by the server and my privacy is under threat, for example.

Solution 9. There is more than one BSD license. It's better to be specific.

Solution 10. My software will be automatically copyrighted. Others will not be able to exercise all the four essential freedoms described in the lecture 1.2.

A.4 Quiz 4

Solution 1.
- It had no economy of scale.
- It was decentralized.

Solution 2. It was decentralized.

Solution 3. In age of a printing press.

Solution 4. It restricted only limited amount of people — publishers.

Solution 5. It is not easy because it shall be enforced against everyone which requires invading people's homes, computers and Internet connections

Solution 6.
- No DRM.
- No EULA.
- Ability to purchase anonymously.

Solution 7.
- Attribution-ShareAlike 4.0 International (CC BY-SA 4.0).
- Attribution 4.0 International (CC BY 4.0).

Solution 8.
- Attribution-NonCommercial 4.0 International (CC BY-NC 4.0)
- Attribution-NoDerivatives 4.0 International (CC BY-ND 4.0)

Solution 9. Which CC license will be used?

Solution 10. Public traded away certain parts of its natural rights that ordinary people were not exercising and in exchange got real benefits of more books being written‘

A.5 Quiz 5

Solution 1. Non-free firmware "blobs" which can be found in Linux kernel.

Solution 2. Education system serves public interest therefore it shall not be favourable to any business.

Solution 3.
- It blocks JavaScript code if it is either non-trivial or non-free.
- It makes it easier to complain about non-free JavaScript to web masters.

Solution 4.
- It blocks Google Analytics.
- It maintains list of free add-ons.
- It contains LibreJS extension to address the JavaScript problem known as "Javascript Trap".

Solution 5. Convert the file to Ogg Vorbis or webm format and find the service to publish it. This service shall deliver video to the users in the format favourable to the free software and should not lead its users to use non-free programs (e.g., non-free JavaScript).

Solution 6.
- They are well-known.
- They are more convenient than non-free GNU/Linux distributions.

Solution 7. There people and powerful organizations which are trying to demonise freedom fighters.That's why it's especially important to state that they are heroes who are fighting for our freedom.

Solution 8.
- It makes it possible to study source code.
- It makes it possible to write small changes in the big programs.
- By studying free software source code the student can know what is bad coding style and how he or she shall not write programs.

Solution 9. Campaign exposing DRM-encumbered devices and media for what they really are. Supporters are working together to eliminate DRM as a threat to innovation in media, the privacy of readers, and freedom for computer users.

Solution 10. Proprietary systems that are jails — they do not allow the user to freely install applications. These systems are platforms for censorship imposed by the company that owns the system.

APPENDIX B

LIST OF ABBREVIATIONS

AACS   Advanced Access Content System

AGPL   GNU Affero General Public License

BSD   Berkeley Software Distribution

CC   Creative Commons

CDMA   Code Division Multiple Access

CIA   Central Intelligence Agency

DMCA   Digital Millennium Copyright Act

DNS   Domain Name System

DRM   Digital Restrictions Management / Digital Rights Management

DVD   Digital Versatile Disc

EU   European Union

EULA   End-User License Agreement

FSF   Free Software Foundation

GFDL   GNU Free Documentation License

GNU   GNU's Not Unix

GPL   GNU General Public License

GPS   Global Positioning System

GSM   Groupe Spécial Mobile

IP   Internet Protocol

ISP   Internet Service Provider

JS   JavaScript

LZW   Lempel-Ziv-Welch

MIT   Massachusetts Institute of Technology

MPEG   Moving Picture Experts Group

MPL   Mozilla Public License

OS   Operating System

USA   United States of America

USB   Universal Serial Bus

APPENDIX C

INDEX

Antiquity, 26
Authorship, 13, 26–28

CDMS, 15
Computer networks, 27

Data Formats
    Flash, 32
    MP*, 32
    Ogg/Vorbis, 21, 32
    QuickTime, 32
    Webm, 32
Digital Society, 12

Easy Changes, 35
Education, 33, 34

Facebook, 32, 34
Four Freedoms, 6, 35
Freedom Fighters, 14, 34

GNU, 32
Google, 34
GPS, 15
GSM, 15

ISP, 14

JavaScript, 32, 33

Knuth, Donald, 20

Licenses, 20
    AGPL, 21
    Apache 2.0, 21
    BSD, 21
    Copyleft, 20
    Copyright, 20, 26, 27
    Creative Commons, 28
    GPL, 20
    MIT, 21
    MPL, 20
    Pushover, 20, 21
    Weak copyleft, 21
    X11, 21

Mobile Phones, 12

Orwell, "1984", 28

Patents, 6
Piracy, 13, 35
Printing Press, 26

RS-232, 15

School, 33
Sharing, 13, 14, 35
Software
    Firmware, 32
    Free, 6, 14, 20, 27, 32, 33
    GNU IceCat, 34
    GNU LibreJS, 33, 34
    GNU/Linux, 32
    GNU/Linux distributions, 6
    Malicious, 6
    MS Windows, 35
    Proprietary, 6, 32
    Skype, 6
    TEX, 20
Swindle, 12, 27, 28, 32, 34

Threats
    Backdoor, 12, 13
    Censorship, 12, 26
    DMCA, 14
    DRM, 6, 12, 14, 28, 32, 35
    Mickey Mouse Copyright Act, 27
    Precarity, 13, 14
    Propaganda, 12, 13, 35
    SaaSS, 13, 21
    Surveillance, 12

University, 33
USB, 15

WikiLeaks, 14

Youtube, 32

www.ingramcontent.com/pod-product-compliance
Lightning Source LLC
Chambersburg PA
CBHW071005290526
45795CB00005B/1785